Happy Coloring!

Heather Land
HEATHER'S ADULT COLORING BOOKS
www.HeatherLandBooks.com

Respectfully dedicated to
ST LOUIS
Birdie Darling
OR
FLY ACROSS THE OCEAN BIRDIE
BEAUTI

William T. Cooper
1995

was looking over some
this delightful afternoon
in perusing your last
welcome missive which
unanswered I feel the
quotation
Being

Spring-Flowers

8

Pieces

S. JADASSOHN

BOOK 1. 75ᶜ   BOOK 2. 75ᶜ

NEW-YORK.
G. SCHIRMER, 35 UNION SQUARE.

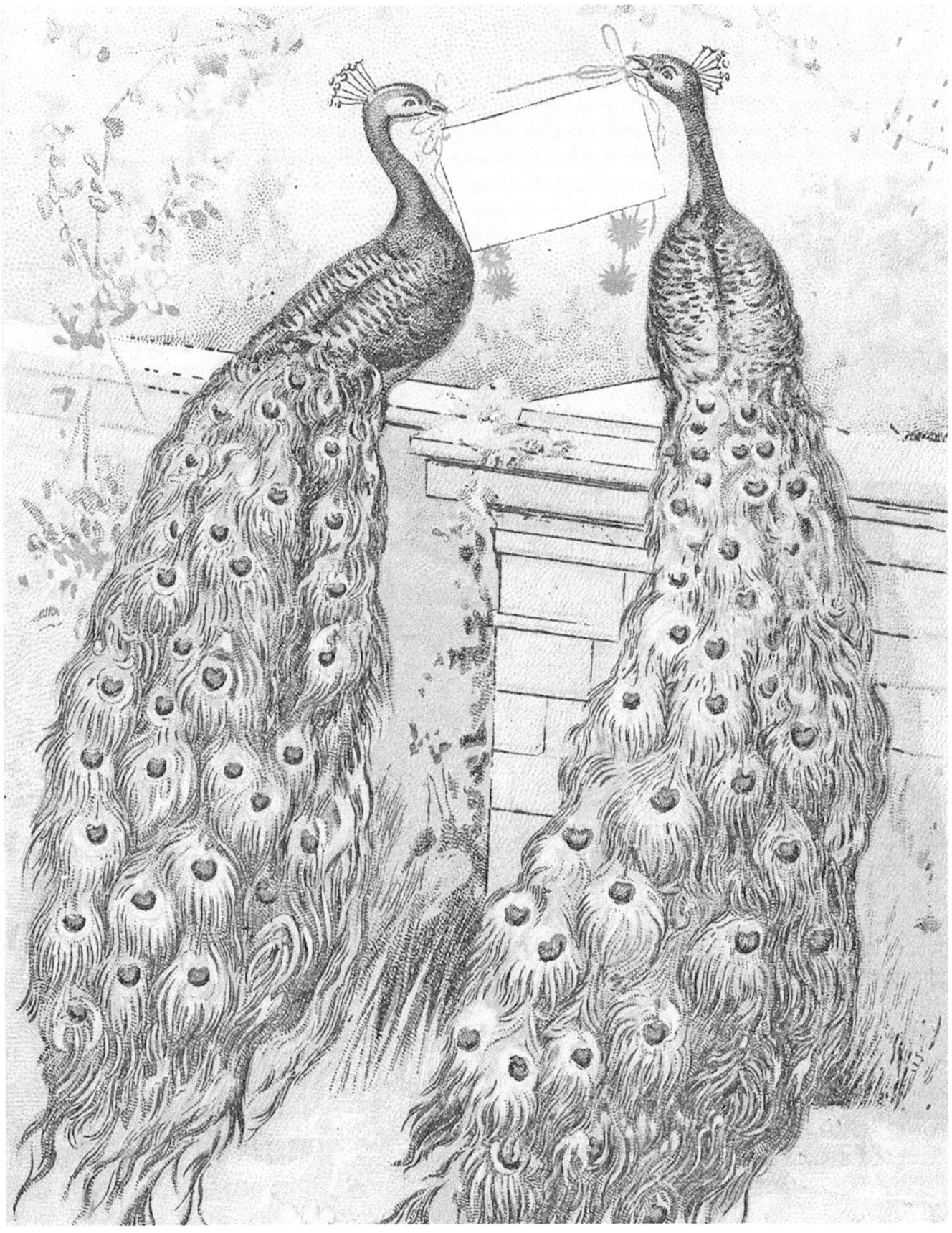

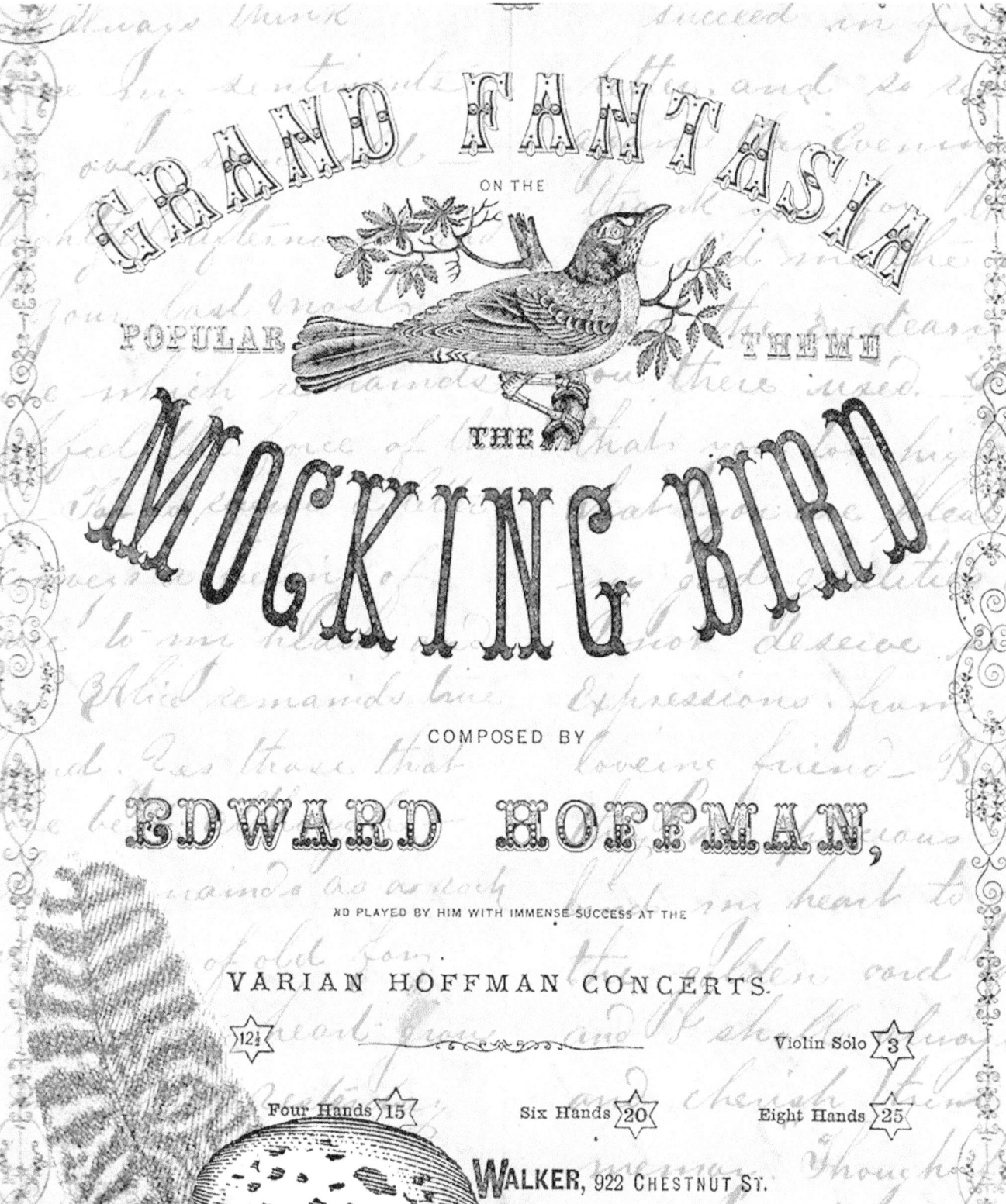

ELECTROTYPED BY   L. JOHNSON & CO. PHILA.

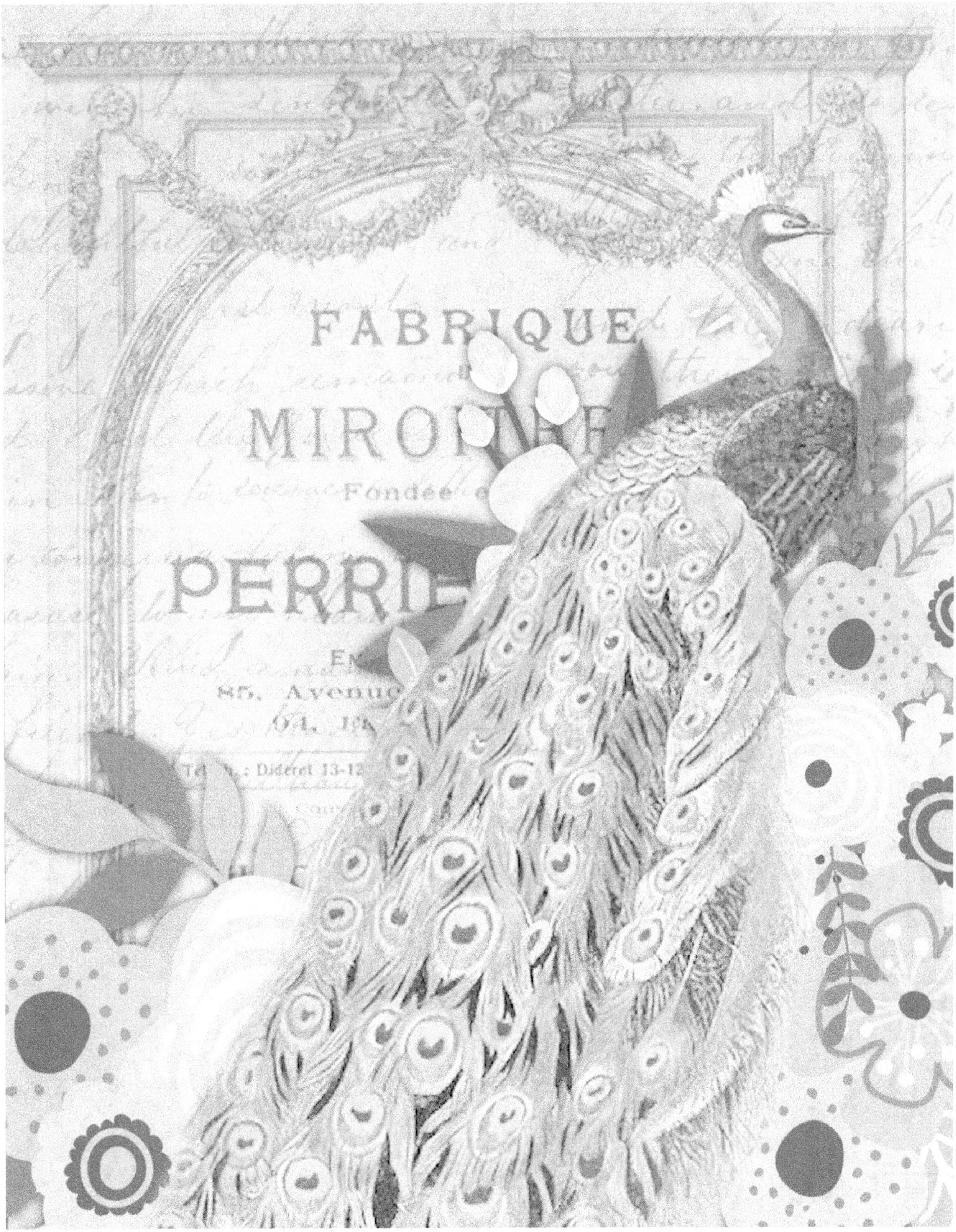
FABRIQUE
Fondée

COLOR TEST SQUARES

TEST YOUR COLORS HERE AND USE THIS
PAGE AS A REFERENCE GUIDE

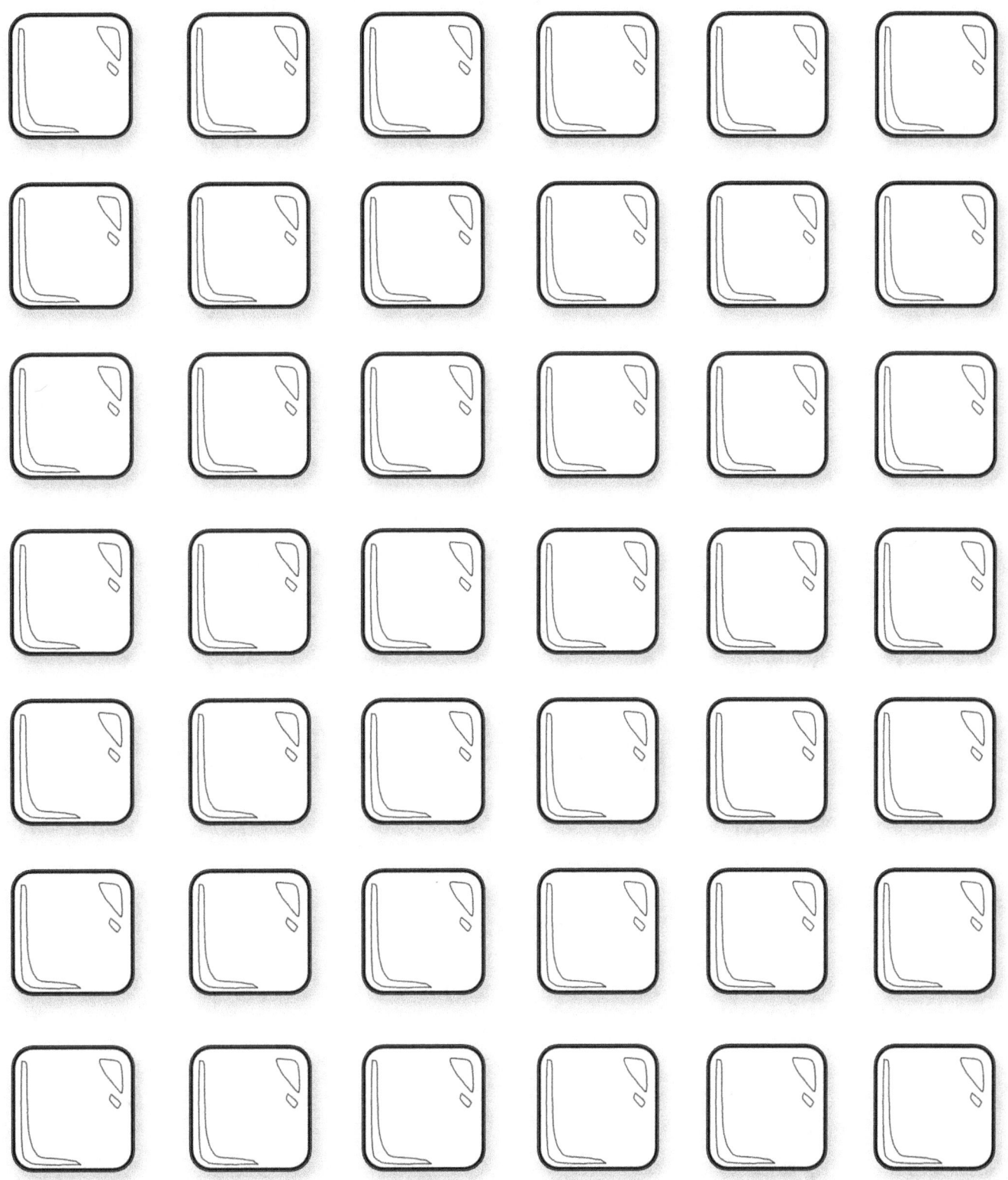

COLOR TEST SQUARES

TEST YOUR COLORS HERE AND USE THIS
PAGE AS A REFERENCE GUIDE

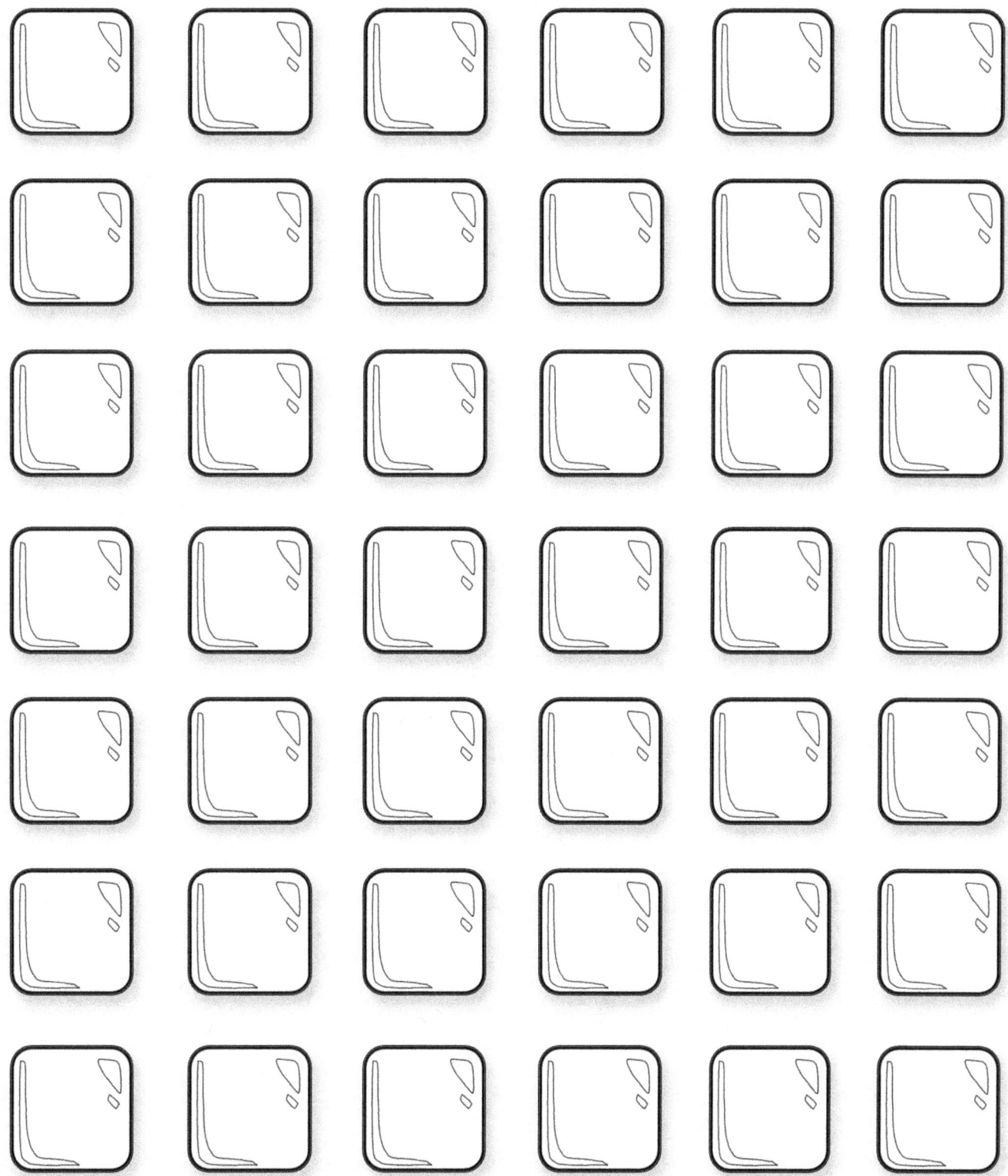

www.ingramcontent.com/pod-product-compliance
Lightning Source LLC
Chambersburg PA
CBHW081416280526
45788CB00009B/3124